MURRA

TOUT · PRÊT

Ancient Murray

Weathered Murray

Murray of Tullibardine

Modern Murray

CLAN
MURRAY

COMPILED BY
Alan McNie

CASCADE PUBLISHING COMPANY
Jedburgh, Scotland

4

Alan McNie, 1980, revised 1983
© Cascade Publishing Company
Rowandene, Belses, Jedburgh, Scotland

ISBN 0 9076145 0 7

Page 1 Explanation:
The illustrated tartan is the ancient Murray, which is preferred by the present Duke of Atholl. The motto on the crest badge means 'Quite ready'. The artist's montage depicts the present clan seat, Blair Castle, and in the foreground is Juniper, the preferred clan plant badge of the Murrays.

Bothwell Castle, very early Murray association he

Bothwell Castle

6

The McIan illustration of Murray as published (mid-19th century) in 'The Clans of the Scottish Highlands'

CLAN
MURRAY

Condensed from Keltie's Scottish Highlands (1879)

The great family of Murray or Moray (occasionally in old deeds Murreff) is supposed to have descended from Freskine (or Friskin), a Fleming who settled in Scotland in the reign of David I (1122 - 1153), and acquired from that monarch the lands of Strathbroch in Linlithgowshire, and of Duffus in Moray.

Friskin's grandson, William de Moravia, married the daughter and heiress of David de Olifard, and was the ancestor of the Morays of Bothwell and Abercairny.

His descendant, the 7th in possession, Sir William Murray of Tullibardine, succeeded to the estates of his family in 1446. He was sheriff of Perthshire, and in 1458 one of the lords named for the administration of justice, who were of the king's daily council. He married Margaret daughter of Sir John Colquhoun of Luss, great chamberlain of Scotland, by whom he had numerous children. According to tradition they had seventeen sons, from whom a great many families of the name of Murray are descended.

The eldest of Tullibardine's seventeen sons, Sir William Murray of Tullibardine, had, with other issue, William, his successor, and Sir Andrew Murray, ancestor of the Viscounts Stormont. His great grandson, Sir William Murray of Tullibardine, was a zealous promoter of the Reformation in Scotland. A document of 1710 concerning the seventeen sons states that: "Sir William Murray of Tullibardine having broke Argyll's face with the hilt of his sword in King James the Sixth's presence, was obliged to leave the kingdom. Afterwards, the king's mails and slaughter cows were not paid, neither could any subject to the realm be able to compel those who were bound to pay them; upon which the king cried out – 'O, if I had Will Murray again, he would soon get my mails and slaughter cows;' to which one standing by replied – 'That if his Majesty would not take Sir William Murray's life, he might return shortly.' The king answered, 'He would be loath to take his life, for he had not another subject like him!' Upon which promise Sir

William Murray returned and got a commission from the king to go to the north, and lift up the mails and the cows, which he speedily did, to the great satisfaction of the king, so that immediately after he was made lord comptroller." This office he obtained in 1565.

His eldest son, Sir John Murray, the twelfth feudal baron of Tullibardine, was brought up with King James, who in 1592 constituted him his master of the household. On 10th July 1606 he was created Earl of Tullibardine. His lordship married Catherine, fourth daughter of David, second Lord Drummond, and died in 1609.

His eldest son William, second Earl of Tullibardine, married Lady Dorothea Stewart, eldest daughter and heir of line of the fifth Earl of Athole of the Stewart family, who died in 1595 without male issue. He eventually, in 1625, petitioned King Charles the First for the earldom of Athole. The king received the petition graciously, and gave his royal word that it should be done. The earl accordingly surrendered the title of Earl of Tullibardine into the king's hands, 1st April 1626, to be conferred on his brother Sir Patrick Murray as a separate dignity, but before the patents could be issued, his lordship died the same year.

His son John, however, obtained in February 1629 the title of Earl of Athole, and thus became the first Earl of the Murray branch, and the earldom of Tullibardine was at the same time granted to Sir Patrick. This Earl of Athole was a zealous royalist, and joined the association formed by the Earl of Montrose for the king at Cumbernauld in January 1641. He died in June 1642. His eldest son John, second Earl of Athole of the Murray family, also faithfully adhered to Charles the First, and was excepted by Cromwell out of his act of grace and indemnity, 12th April 1654, when he was only about nineteen years of age. At the Restoration, he was sworn hereditary office of sheriff of Fife, and in 1663 was appointed justice general of Scotland. In 1670 he was constituted captain of the king's guards, in 1672 keeper of the privy seal, and in 1673, an extraordinary lord of session. In 1670 he succeeded to the earldom of Tullibardine on the death of James, fourth earl of the new creation, and was created Marquis of Athole in 1676. He increased the power of his family by his marriage with Lady Amelia Sophia Stanley, third daughter of the seventh Earl of Derby, beheaded for his loyalty in 1651. Through her mother, Charlotte de la Tremouille, she was related in blood to the Emperor of Germany, the kings of France and Spain, the Prince of Orange, the Duke of Savoy, and most of the principal families of Europe; and by her the family of Athole acquired the seignory of the Isle of Man, and also large property in that island.

John, the second Marquis and first Duke of Athole, then designated Lord Murray, was one of the commissioners for inquiring into the massacre of Glencoe in 1693. He was created a peer in his father's lifetime, by the title of Earl of Tullibardine, Viscount of Glenalmond, and Lord Murray, for life, in 1696, and in 1703 he was

Scone Palace, a senior cadet of Atholl is the Earl of Mansfie

Scone Palace

appointed lord privy seal. On the 30th of July of that year, immediately after his father's death, he was created Duke of Athole by Queen Ann, and invested with the order of the Thistle. He died in 1724, having been twice married.

His eldest son John, Marquis of Tullibardine, was killed at the battle of Malplaquet in 1709. His second son William, who succeeded his brother, was the Marquis of Tullibardine who acted a prominent part in both the Scottish rebellions of the 18th century. In 1745 he accompanied Prince Charles Edward to Scotland, and landed with him at Borodale on 25th July, He was styled Duke of Athole by the Jacobites. After the battle of Culloden he fled to the west, intending to embark for the Isle of Mull, but being unable, from the bad state of his health, to bear the fatigue of travelling under concealment, he surrendered on the 27th April to Mr Buchanan of Drummakill, a Stirlingshire gentleman. He was conveyed to London and committed to the Tower, where he died in the following July.

James, the second Duke of Athole, was the third son of the first duke. He was married first to Jean, widow of James Lannoy of Hammersmith, and sister of Sir John Frederick, by whom he had a son and two daughters; secondly to Jane, daughter of John Drummond of Megginch, who had no issue. Charlotte, his younger daughter , succeeded on his death, which took place in 1764, to the barony of Strange and the sovereignty of the Isle of Man. She married her cousin, John Murray, eldest son of Lord George Murray, fifth son of the first duke, and the celebrated general of the forces of Prince Charles Edward in 1745. Though Lord George was attained by parliament for his share in the rebellion, his son was allowed to succeed his uncle and father in law as third duke, and in 1765 he and his duchess disposed of their sovereignty of the Isle of Man to the British govern-ment for seventy thousand pounds, reserving, however, their landed interest in the island. He was succeeded by his eldest son John, fourth duke, who in 1786 was created Earl Strange and Baron Murray of Stanley, in the peerage of the United Kingdom. The fourth duke was succeeded by his eldest son John, who was for many years a recluse, and died single in 1846. His next brother, James, a major-general in the army, was created a peer of the United Kingdom, as Baron Glenlyon of Glenlyon, in 1821. He married the second daughter of the Duke of Northumber-land, and by her had two sons and two daughters. He died in 1837. His eldest son, George, became, on the death of his uncle in 1846, sixth Duke of Athole. He died in 1864, and was succeeded by his only son, John, seventh Duke of Athole, who inherited the barony of Percy and several co-heirships on the death of his great uncle Algernon, fourth Duke of Northumberland, in 1865.

Murray Country
DETAIL MAP OVERLEAF

The map used below and on the following page is intended basically as a pictorial reference. It is accurate enough, however, to be correlated with a current map. The clan boundaries are only marginally correct. No precise boundaries were kept in early times and territories were fluctuating frequently.

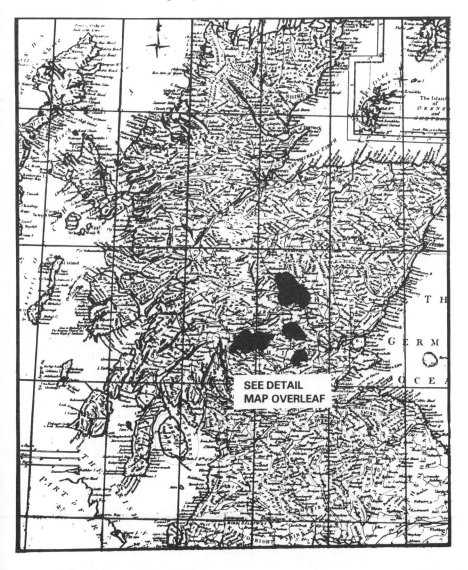

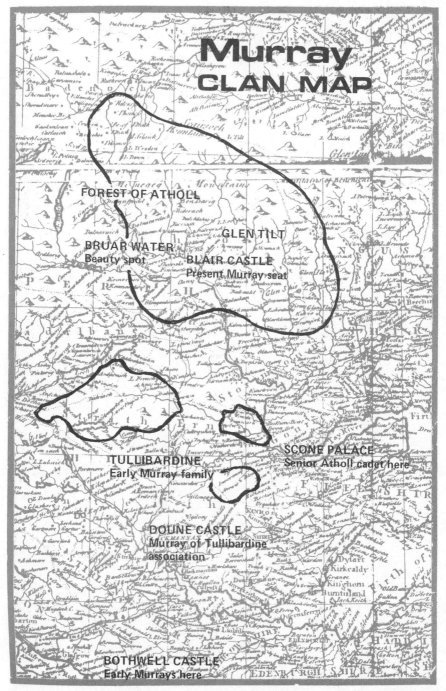

Murray
CLAN MAP

FOREST OF ATHOLL

GLEN TILT

BRUAR WATER
Beauty spot

BLAIR CASTLE
Present Murray seat

TULLIBARDINE
Early Murray family

SCONE PALACE
Senior Atholl cadet here

DOUNE CASTLE
Murray of Tullibardine
association

BOTHWELL CASTLE
Early Murrays here

Bruar Water, where the falls have thrilled for centuries

Bruar Water

Murray Associated Names

Associated names have a hazy history. Sometimes they had more than one origin; also clouding the precise location of a particular surname might be that name's proscription or of course a migrant population. Even the spelling of surnames was subject to great variations, shifting from usually Latin or Gaelic and heeding rarely to consistent spelling. In early records there can be several spellings of the same name. Undoubtedly contributing to this inconsistency is the handwriting in official records, which was often open to more than one spelling interpretation.

With regard to the 'Mac' prefix, this was, of course, from the Gaelic meaning, son of. It wasn't long before it was abbreviated to 'Mc' or 'M', until we have reached the position now where there are more 'Mc's' than 'Mac's'.

BALNEAVES   From nameplace in Angus. Some of these Balneaves became adherents of the Murrays in Atholl. Henry Benese recorded in Jedburgh, 1541. John Balnaves, scribe to Assembly of Perth, 1587.

DUNBAR From nameplace in Lothian. Also used by Crinan, Dunkeld landowner, whose grandfather probably Dunchad, abbot of Dunkeld, killed in 965 and either his mother or grandmother could have been a daughter of a king of the isles. The lands of Glenkens and Mochrem (Galloway) acquired by Dunbars, 1368.

FLEMING   A Flanders native. About 1150 Baldwin the Fleming was sheriff of Lanark. In 1245 Adam Flamanke acted as witness in Annandale. Bartholomew Flamang witnessed in 1258 argument involving Bishop of Moray.

MACMURRAY, MORAY, MURRIE Variants of Murray.

PIPER, PYPER   Name derived from occupation. Also common Perth name. Schir Johne Pipar, recorded as Dunkeld chaplain in 1546. William Pyper was Perth town councillor in 1567. Some Pypers were adherents of Murray of Aberscorse.

SMAIL, SMALE, SMALL, SMEALL, SMEALLE   A canon of Glasgow in early 14th century was Richard Smale or Small. About 1338 Thomas Smale was a Roxburgh witness. Simo Smale was an Ellon, Aberdeenshire businessman, 1402. At the time of the 1745 rebellion the Smalls and variants of that name were followers of the Duke of Atholl.

SPALDING   From nameplace, Spalding, Lincolnshire. First Scottish appearance of name likely Radulphus Spalding of Caterline, Kincardineshire, who was charter witness, 1225. Peter de Spalding, a Berwick burgess, received lands in Angus for services rendered to Robert the Bruce, 1319. A branch of the Spaldings in the 1745 rebellion fought under the Duke of Atholl.

Lord George Murray

Scottish Roots

The maps below and opposite are intended to show the early occurrence of associated names with clan affiliation. These names also appear with the pertinent historical detail under the associated names on page 14. An historic map has been used as a pictorial background but locations can be fairly easily transposed to a current map.

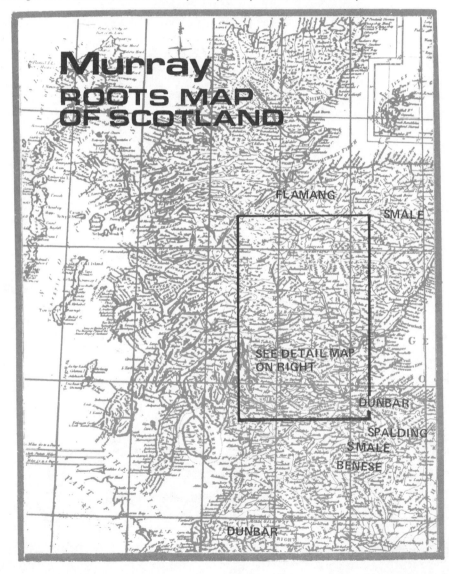

Murray
ROOTS MAP
OF SCOTLAND

FLAMANG

SMALE

SEE DETAIL MAP
ON RIGHT

DUNBAR

SPALDING
SMALE

BENESE

DUNBAR

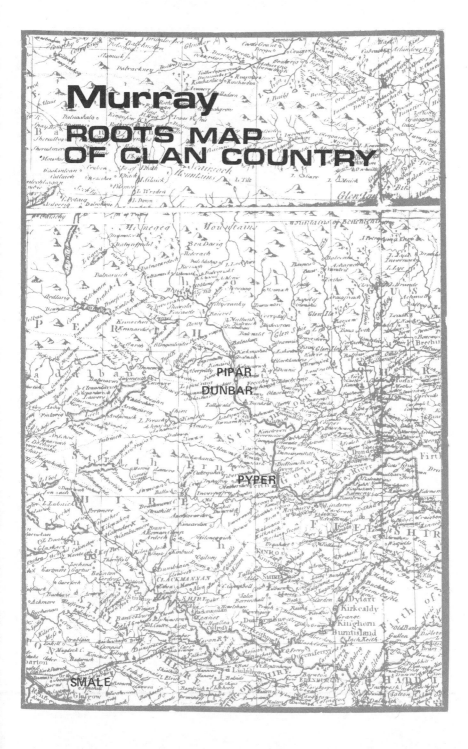

Murray
ROOTS MAP
OF CLAN COUNTRY

PIPAR
DUNBAR

PYPER

SMALE

Doune Castle was important in early clan history

Atholl Highlanders and their chieftain fought at Culloden

Nova Scotia (New Scotland), strong scenic and cultural links with the homeland

WANDERLUST

For centuries Scots have travelled the globe seeking challenge and fulfilment. A glance through the telephone directories of most countries will uncover Scottish presence. Not so well known are the origins of the Scot. His ancestors came from many diverse places.

About the 6th century Irish settlers from Antrim founded settlements in Argyllshire. These Celtic immigrants, called Scots, provided the nation's name. However they were by no means the only people inhabiting Scotland at that time. For several centuries previously the Picts had controlled much of the northern expanse. These earliest settlers were of unknown origin but they may have come from Sythia.

Also filling in the Scottish mosiac were a branch of the Britons from England who were forced into Strathclyde by some of the Angles. This race, whose name was adopted for England, arrived by the North Sea.

Another race who left their influential stamp on many of Scotland's highest offices were the Normans. From the 8th to the 10th centuries Norsemen extensively raided and settled in the Orkney and Shetland Islands where Norse influences are still highly meaningful today. Other intrepid Norsemen splashed ashore at all parts of the mainland coast with the exception of the south-east.

These races, with their different languages and customs, provided a hetrogeneous mix, which almost miraculously became a Scottish nation, resolute and proud for the most part of their national identity. The melding of the diffuse elements is even more remarkable when it is remembered that the eventual synthesis of Scotland occurred in spite of a formidable linguistic, cultural, economic and geographical divide. The great schism was loosely termed Highlands and Lowlands.

THE SCOTTISH DIVIDE

In fact the Lowlands encompassed the entire east coast of Scotland and penetrated even the most northerly section, the orkney and Shetland Islands. The legitimately-designed Lowland area included all parts of Scotland south of the Forth-Clyde inlets, with all other parts of Scotland categorized as Highland. Gaelic emerged as the language of the Highlands, and Lowland Scots that of the Lowlands.

With Scotland's development as an agrarian economy the geographical divide became a fundamental force in dividing the nation into two widely differing areas of agricultural productivity. The thin soil of the Highlands, coupled with seemingly incessant rain and wind, produced a harsh environment that made even subsistence farming difficult. Contrasting with the hostile environment was the Lowlands, with generally drier weather and fertile soil.

Psychologically the Highlander was inhibited by the tortuous coastline that provided at the time a westward vista to no known promised land. The Lowlanders could fortunately look to a largely hospitable coastline as a base for continental trading. Another advantage for the Lowlands was the ancillary benefits from nearby burghs and institutions, which had limited benefit initially but gathered importance as the centuries passed.

THE CLAN SYSTEM

The Lowlanders had a clan system of their own, with the chief and their landlords sharing a name, but the tenant became increasingly less dependent on the chief for matters such as the maintenance of law and order. The relationship became essentially commercial as time passed. Centralized authority was exercised more easily in the Lowlands, as growing opportunities within the populated areas created a flow from countryside to burgh, which gathered considerable pace with economic change.

Through many harsh centuries the Highlanders functioned within a clan system that generally provided basic humanitarian and economic benefit to tenants, often living in isolated glens. the clan chieftains rented large tracts of land to tacksmen who in turn parcelled the land off to tenants who paid them rent.

Besides agrarian pursuits, the other necessary cog in the clan organizational machinery was a formidable militia. This independent military force mustered the tenants for doing battle against other clans or the English. When attacking other clans they were usually intent on returning with booty. The militia of course had to defend itself against attack.

When law and order became widely enforced through the Highlands, some clans were unable to provide enough food from their meagre soil resources to support all their tenants. The insufficiency provided one spark that would combine with many others to fire the disintegration of the clan system.

THE SCOTTISH MONARCHY

Concurrent with the clan system, and indeed its creator, was the Scottish monarchy, which amazingly survived although beset with several internal and external pressures. The bloody and battered lineage was sustained for many

Bannockburn

centuries. Pressure to be absorbed into England with its similar language and customs would have proved irresistible to many nations. English military thrusts, when successful against Wallace, did not dampen the nationalist fervour of the Scot. That was proven beyond any doubt when, in 1314, Robert the Bruce rallied 10,000 clansmen to an ignominious defeat of the English at Bannockburn. Scottish nationalism still persisted even when Scotland's and England's parliaments were united in 1707.

The parliamentary system gave representation to both countries. Distinctive institutions such as law, church and education were retained, along with a unique cultural heritage. These Scottish elements were buttressed by the canny, quiet resolve of the Scottish psyche that has developed through well over a millenium. Within Scotland today the majority of people consistently want greater automony in managing their own affairs, indicating that the essence of the Scottish identity and self-awareness remains undiluted.

COLLAPSE OF THE CLAN SYSTEM

At the same time as central authority was stabilizing at the beginning of the 18th century, the clan system was, not surprisingly, entering into its death throes. One reason, of course, for disintegration was the declining power of the chief over his clansmen, which was supplanted by other agencies.

Another telling blow was the introduction of sheep into the Highlands. Sheep required far fewer farm workers than cattle, while inexpensively satisfying the needs of burgeoning town populations for food and clothing. The short-lived kelp industry offered only a temporary respite to the rapid depopulation of the destitute Highlands.

Thus the overwhelming defeat at Culloden in 1746 merely brought to a head matters that had been festering for centuries. To wage battle at Culloden, a small force of 5,000 clansmen was mustered when 300,000 people lived in the Highlands at the time. Far more clans were either not represented or fought on the government side.

Following Culloden the already faltering clan system collapsed. This system at its best was a communal attack on a generally harsh environment and unfriendly neighbours. At times it wavered from within, with family feuds fuelled by the proximity and pervasiveness of communal life. Also some chieftains demanded more than a fair share of a meagre lot. Stability was usually maintained, however, through selfless acts of the highest order: the needy were treated with the greatest magnanimity; unrestrained acts of kindness came from every stratum in the clan structure. Today's fascination with clan origins among descendants many generations removed, is usually attributed to a search for identity. But another motivation could be that we live in a world where concern is increasingly for self rather than neighbour. The clan system at its best showed a simple but profound functioning of kith and kin, with care for one another.

ANGLO-SCOTS

The depopulation of the Highlands occurred on a massive scale, with Highlanders, in traditional Scottish fashion, spreading near and far. Some headed for the Lowlands, but for many that proved to be only a stepping stone. For some Scots infected with wanderlust the most important road in Scotland was the road south to England. They believed greater opportunities existed in a more prosperous and populous land. In the first half of the 16th century 3,000 Scots settled in England.

Right through into the twentieth century this flow has been maintained. At times it has reached tidal proportions. Between 1925-35 possibly 60,000 Scots took the road south to England. Over the centuries this brain drain has included Adam Smith, Thomas Carlyle, Sir James Barrie, Robert and John Adam, Arthur Conan Doyle and several British prime ministers.

The Continent has long been a magnet for the wandering Scot. Students for many years have studied there, particularly in France. Some 400 Scottish names were recorded at the University of Paris between 1519 and 1615. Ecclesiastics were also prevalent in Europe. In the 15th century large numbers of Scottish soldiers supported their French friends of the Auld Alliance. Workers of all kinds—merchant seamen, craftsmen, and pedlars—have been recorded in many European countries, with large numbers settling in the Low Countries, particularly Holland.

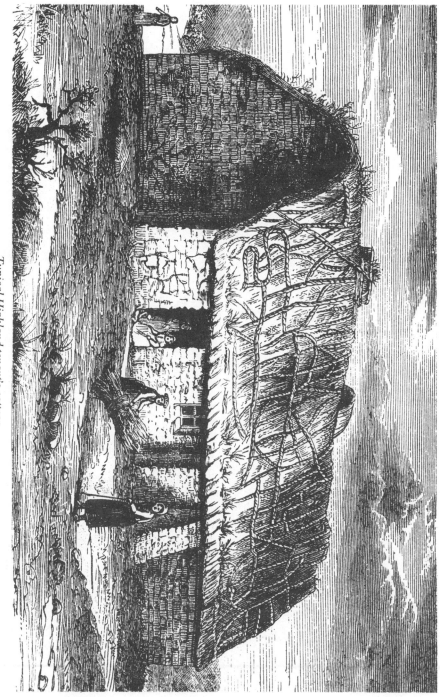

Typical Highland tenant's cottage

Scottish artist David Allan (1744-1796) shows interior of a tenant's period dwelling

SCOTS-AMERICANS

Scots—both Highlanders and Lowlanders—set sail for America in their thousands during the latter part of the 18th century—for the years 1763-75 it could be as high as 25,000. By later standards this was a mere trickle but for that period it could be designated the first immigration wave. Cape Fear Valley in North Carolina, the Mohawk and Upper Hudson valleys in New York, and Attamaha valley in Georgia received the bulk of the Scots.

Even before this large influx some Scots were making notable contributions to their adopted land. Clergyman James Blair founded William and Mary College in 1693. He later became governor of Virginia. Scot Andrew Hamilton was another governor—of New Jersey. John Campbell (1653-1728) was appointed postmaster of Boston, but his real claim to fame was publishing the first newspaper that had been printed in North America, Boston Newsletter (1704).

These three Scots typified the interests of many other emigrant Scots: education, politics and journalism. The exodus from the Highlands was triggered by two other developments, which had considerable bearing on emigration to America. Due to a changed system of Highland land tenure, the tacksmen were being squeezed out. Being resourceful businessmen, they saw an opportunity in America to both organize and lead a settlement. Tenant farmers were also being forced out of the Highlands by huge rent increases.

One sizeable group of Scots should be taken into consideration, particularly at the time of the American Revolution. These were the Ulster Scots, who settled in Northern Ireland in the 17th century. Their descendants accounted for a significant proportion of the 189,000 people of Scottish origin recorded in America in 1790. Their position in the American War of Independence was largely anti-British.

Settlers from Scotland as a whole did not support the revolution and many emigrated to Canada, although there were notable exceptions. John Witherspoon was a framer of the Declaration of Independence. Naturally enough, as an aftermath of the revolution Scottish emigration declined for a few years. However between 1820 and 1950 Scots emigrating to America numbered at least 800,000. Obviously among that number there were those who returned home, but when it is remembered that the population of Scotland did not reach five million until the second quarter of this century, it is a considerable portion. During that period possibly the two most important figures of Scottish birth were Andrew Carnegie and Alexander Graham Bell.

In America as elsewhere the Scots have assimilated well, but nevertheless their heritage has not been forgotten. The staggering proliferation of Highland games, pipe bands, and clan associations across America ensures that the vitality and appeal of the Scottish tradition will be nurtured by Scots and their descendants for years to come.

Lanarkshire, Scotland, he received elementary schooling before working in coal mines at the age of ten. He emigrated to Pittsburgh, eventually becoming President of United Mine Workers. In 1940 he became president of Congress of Industrial Organisations. He fought for increased standards of living, pensions and benefits and fair treatment of workers.

SCOTS-CANADIANS

The first groups of Scots to arrive in Canada needed indomitable spirit. Those, who arrived as destitute Highlanders in the present-day Maritimes, found little to better their desperate condition. One such group arrived in 1773 at Pictou, Nova Scotia, on the Hector; the plucky passengers waded ashore behind the reassuring skirl of the pipes.

Another wave of Highlanders settled in Upper Canada (Ontario) following the American Revolution. Of particular interest was the Glengarry settlement in the township of the same name, which was settled by many of the Clan MacDonnell of Glengarry, Invernesshire. Members of other clans spread themselves through many parts of Ontario including these notable Scottish areas: Perth, Lanark County; MacNab Township; Guelph; Talbot; Middlesex, Huron and Bruce Counties.

A large number of United Empire Loyalists also arrived in Ontario following the American Revolution, including some of the many Scots who were crown supporters at the time of the revolution. No account of Scottish pioneers would be complete without referring to the heroic and selfless efforts of Lord Selkirk to found an early 19th century Red River settlement (for impoverished Highlanders) in Manitoba. His laudable plans were brutally thwarted several times by traders of the North West Company.

To the east, especially in Ontario, conditions were relatively easier for the rapidly increasing numbers of immigrants from 1815-1850. Ontario was still attracting the lion's share. The Scot, adventurous as ever, continued to form an exceptional percentage of the new arrivals. By 1871 there were approximately 550,000 Scots in Canada, while from vastly more populous England there were slightly over 700,000.

The West was won by settlers at the end of the 19th century and the beginning of the 20th century, with still large numbers of Scots spreading their influence across the prairies. The unique Scottish heritage is alive and well in Canada, with a difference in emphasis between Nova Scotia and the rest of Canada. In Nova Scotia the roots, which are Gaelic, go back much further. Gaelic is still taught at college level on Cape Breton Island. The Scottish traditions of Nova Scotia are based on their Highland heritage. In the rest of Canada the Scottish traditions are wider based, with Burns Suppers, for example, being very popular. Some Scots who have left indelible marks on Canada's path to greatness are: Canada's first prime minister, Sir John A. Macdonald; inventor Alexander Graham Bell; explorer-trader Sir Alexander Mackenzie; publisher-politician George Brown.

Reproduction of drawing
by Scottish artist, David Allan (1744-96).

Poor Father of 20 Children

David Allan graphically illustrates a major Highland problem: over-population

From earliest days the Murrays have contributed significantly to Canadian development. Among the prominent personalities was James Murray (1721-1794) born at Ballencrieff, Scotland the youngest son of Alexander 4th Lord Elibank. He entered the army in 1740 and was one of Wolfe's brigadiers in 1759 during the siege of Quebec. In 1760 he was military governor of Quebec and in 1764 the first civil governor.

SCOTS-AUSTRALIANS

The first flood of emigrants to Australia were convicts, who were sent between 1788-1820 to New South Wales and Tasmania. Among these convicts were political as well as criminal prisoners. Some of the political prisoners were 18th century reformers, who had corresponded with French revolutionaries. Today such persons could well be members of parliament or clergymen. And among the criminal prisoners were probably those who were improperly convicted as well as those who had committed a petty crime.

It should be stated that sometimes Scottish political convicts were allowed to manage their own farms or pursue a trade. Free settlers, enticed by the large fertile parts of Australia being opened, quickly changed the large proportion of convicts compared with free settlers. By 1828 those who chose to emigrate to New South Wales numbered 4,673, compared with 7,500 freed convicts and 15,600 still in bondage. The number of free settlers had more than quadrupled in nine years. One of the earliest free settlers was Robert Campbell (1769-1846) who was a Sydney merchant in 1798. Two successive Scottish governors—Lachlan Macquire and Sir Thomas Brisbane—may have helped Scottish emigration.

Scots were prominent in further expansion in the 1830s, this time in Western Australia with the Swan River Colony. Another Scot, Angus MacMillan founded the Grippsland area, ideal for grazing. Further advancement was made in Queensland by Scot, Thomas Petrie, who opened up this area. In Victoria, Scottish farmers succeeded in a big way. Massive acreages for raising cattle and sheep were owned by many Highlanders, who became very wealthy. Neil Campbell, for example, claimed that within two years of arriving from Mull in 1838, he earned £1000 per annum.

The discovery of gold in New South Wales and Victoria created a dramatic upturn in Scottish emigration to Australia. For those who didn't strike it rich, farming was still expanding at an amazing rate; ancillary employment associated with gold mining also triggered thousands of jobs.

Scottish strength in Australia is exemplified by the 100,000 Scots reported there at the turn of the century. Two Scottish descendants achieved Australia's highest office: Prime Ministers Sir Robert Gordon Menzies and (John) Malcolm Fraser, with Mr Fraser preferring his Scottish given name. Particularly strong Scots-Australian traditions are pipe bands and Scottish country dancing.

R. R. McIan's Victorian illustration from 'Clans of the Scottish Highlands'. Although bound for Canada, the rueful appearance of this emigrant could apply to any destination. Some emigrants, sailing in squalid conditions, failed to reach their new homeland alive and those that did often encountered formidable difficulties.

Australian affairs have been shaped by Murrays for many generations. Among the notables was Reginald A. F. Murray (1846-1925) born in Perthshire, Scotland. He qualified in Australia as a mining surveyor and devoted himself to surveying unexplored Gippsland. Murray investigated brown coal deposit that became important to Victoria's economy and did much prospecting work.

SCOTS-NEW ZEALANDERS

With the purchase of huge parcels of land in 1839, the New Zealand Land Company paved the way for large scale settlement of New Zealand by British immigrants. Between 1839-44, a large number of Scots were aboard the 63 boats that landed from Britain. Getting an early start were 150 Scots who landed at Port Nicholson, on the extreme south coast of the North Island. Other Scots spread out to many other parts of New Zealand. Included in those settlers were a doctor and an engineer, neither of whom followed their profession but elected to become sheep farmers, which provided ample financial compensation.

Otago, in the southern part of the South Island, was to have a Free Church of Scotland settlement organized on a very rigid basis. As with other overly-controlled overseas settlements they encountered many difficulties. As part of the settlement plan the tower of Dunedin was founded. Today the Scots influence there remains on the street signs, with many of Edinburgh's most famous street names found there. The discovery of gold in 1861 in Otago brought in the 'gold rush brigade', which provided a short-term spur to the economy.

But long-term prosperity was found by farming in Otago as well as many other parts of New Zealand. Successful farming, of course, boosted the whole economy, which in turn produced thousands of jobs. Many of these were filled by Scots emigrants in the latter part of the 19th century. By 1901 there were 48,000 Scots living in New Zealand, compared with 110,000 English, proportionately a much larger Scottish presence than English. New Zealand today maintains many Scottish traditions, with particular emphasis on Caledonian societies and an exceptionally large number of pipe bands.

Perhaps Scotland's most famous son was Peter Fraser, who was born (in 1884) in Fearn, Ross and Cromarty, of humble origin. From 1940 this dedicated Prime Minister guided New Zealand through the demanding wartime and postwar period.

The best loved of many Scottish traditions observed world-wide is surely the singing of Auld Lang Syne, notable at Hogmanay (New Year's Eve), but also on many occasions when Scots and those of any other nationality familiar with Burns famous adaptation are gathered together in good fellowship.

ACKNOWLEDGEMENTS

We are indebted to staff members of the Hawick Library and Scottish Room, Edinburgh City Libraries for their generous assistance. Research work done by Barbara Blackburn has proved valuable and thorough.